Georgia O'Keeffe

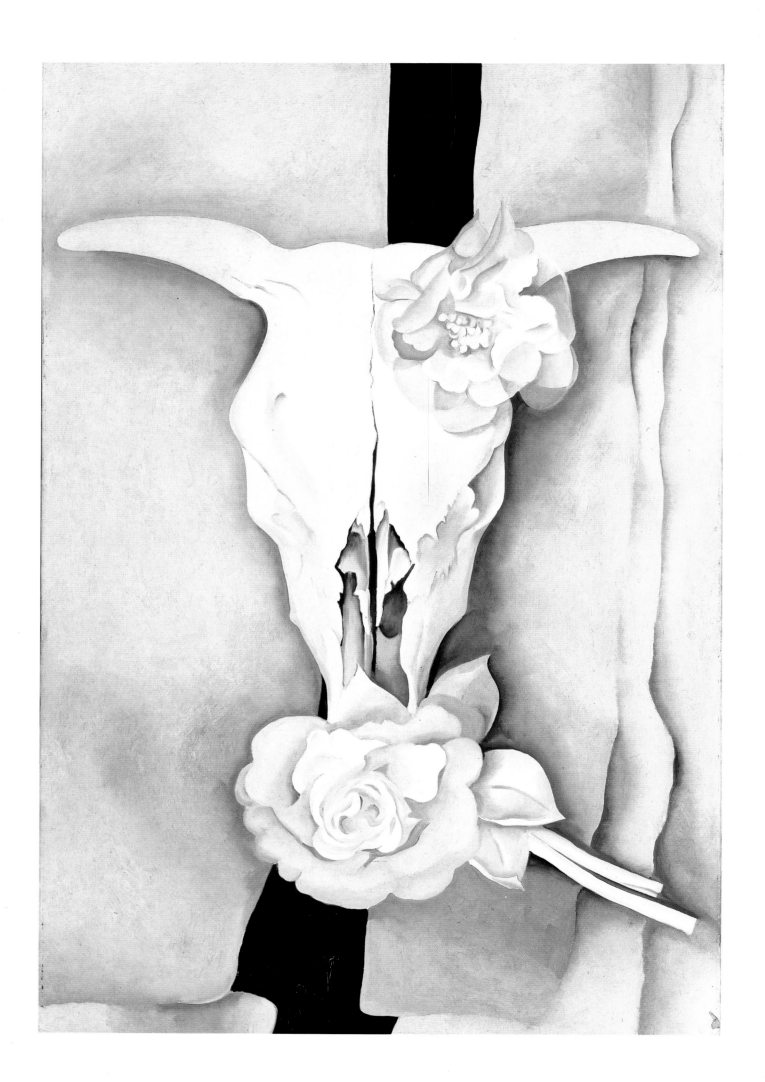

Georgia O'Keeffe

Elizabeth Montgomery

GREENWICH EDITIONS

This edition published by
Greenwich Editions
10 Blenheim Court
Brewery Road
London N7 9NT
England

Published by
Brompton Books Corp.
15 Sherwood Place
Greenwich, CT 06830
USA

ISBN 0-86288-245-1

Printed in Spain

This edition published 1998

Acknowledgments
The publisher and author would like to thank the following people who
helped in the preparation of this book: Design 23; Susan Bernstein, the
editor; and Sara Dunphy, the picture editor.

Page 1:
Georgia O'Keeffe in 1962.

Page 2:
Skull with Calico Roses
1931, oil on canvas, 35.8 × 24 in.
Gift of Georgia O'Keeffe, 1947,
The Art Institute of Chicago, Chicago, IL.

Pages 4-5:
Barn with Snow
1934, oil on canvas, 16 × 28 in.
Gift of Mr. and Mrs. Norton S. Walbridge.
San Diego Museum of Art,
San Diego, CA

CONTENTS

Georgia O'Keeffe the Artist

When Georgia O'Keeffe died in 1986, at the age of ninety-eight, *The New York Times* described her as "the undisputed doyenne of American painting and a leader, with her husband, Alfred Stieglitz, of a crucial phase in the development and dissemination of American modernism." It is almost safe to say that without these two titans there would have been no American modernism movement. Like the other giants who were trained in European methods and sensibilities, O'Keeffe and Stieglitz strove to create a truly American art that looked at the natural landscape of the still unsettled country and tried to portray it in a manner that was unmistakably American. Like architect Frank Lloyd Wright, composer Aaron Copland and dancer Martha Graham, Stieglitz and especially O'Keeffe lived to a great age. And this longevity, in a way, gave their new art a chance to develop and thrive within their lifetimes, so that when the originators of each field died, it was hard to remember a time when people and art had been different.

When Georgia O'Keeffe was born the country was less than 115 years old and entering a period of unquestioned optimism. The American Civil War was a recent memory as was the settling of such midwestern towns as Sun Prairie, Wisconsin, her birthplace. O'Keeffe's family background was diverse and somewhat unusual. Georgia's parents, Ida Ten Eyck Totto and Francis Calyxtus O'Keeffe were married in 1884. Ida Totto was the daughter of a Hungarian count who had been exiled from his own country following the abortive revolution of 1848. Ida's mother was a descendant of a Dutch judge in New York and of Edward Fuller, one of the signers of the Mayflower Compact. Francis O'Keeffe was the son of a wool merchant in Ireland. Francis and Ida's first child, Francis, was born in 1885. Their first daughter, Georgia, was born November 15, 1887. She was followed by four more girls: Anita, Ida, Catherine and Claudia, and another boy, Alexis. It was not unusual to have seven children in a family in the late nineteenth century. But the fact that all of them survived to adulthood might be considered a matter for congratulations. The family circle also included Jane Wyckoff Varney, Georgia's great aunt, who had been widowed early. The presence of another adult woman in the household freed young Georgia from the usual role of an eldest sister, that of perennial babysitter.

According to O'Keeffe, her first memory was of light, sitting on a patchwork quilt and large white pillows. She remembered the fabric patterns and the color of a woman's hair. She also had a later memory of feeling the warm soft ridges of earth made by the wheels of buggies going past their drive. It is not improbable that even at a very early age Georgia O'Keeffe had an unusual sense of color and shape.

The first drawing she could remember making was of a man bending over. "The fact that . . . I tried to draw him bending over makes me think that I must have drawn many figures standing straight . . . . When I had the man with his legs only bent at the hips he just wasn't balanced right. I turned the

Georgia O'Keeffe with her painting *Horse's Skull with White Rose* at the 1931 exhibition at Alfred Stieglitz's An American Place.

paper bag around and saw that he did look right as a man lying on his back with his feet straight up in the air.''

Several years later the young O'Keeffe girls took drawing lessons from a woman in Sun Prairie, who tried to teach them perspective, using the Prang Drawing System. Georgia remembered drawing a spray of oats that she thought was ''pretty good, compared with the drawing in the book.''

When she was thirteen Georgia was sent to boarding school, to the Academy of the Sacred Heart in Madison. Here again she ran up against the conflict between what was expected and her own feeling for art. She was instructed to make a charcoal sketch of a plaster cast of a baby's hand. She used heavy dark lines in creating a small drawing. She was criticized for using the dark lines and for its small size. For the rest of the year she obeyed, and drew everything ''a little lighter and a little larger than I really thought it should be.''

The following year she and her brother Francis attended the high school in Madison. The art teacher there was a woman Georgia disliked personally. ''Holding a Jack-in-the-pulpit high, she pointed out the strange shapes and variations in color — from the deep, almost black earthy violet through all the greens, from the pale whitish green in the flower through the heavy green of the leaves . . . I had seen many Jacks before, but this was the first time I remember examining a flower. I was a little annoyed at being interested because I didn't like the teacher. But maybe she started me looking at things — looking very carefully at details.''

By this time, Georgia was sure she wanted to be an artist, although she didn't know what sort. ''I decided that the only thing I could do that was nobody else's business was to paint. I could do as I chose because no one would care.'' When the O'Keeffe family moved to Williamsburg, Virginia, in the early years of the twentieth century, Georgia was sent to the Chatham Protestant Episcopal Institute. The principal, Elizabeth May Willis, who was also the art teacher, recognized Georgia's talent and allowed her to freely use the studio, experiment with watercolors and go for long walks in the nearby woods.

After graduating from Chatham, Georgia was encouraged by her mother and Mrs. Willis to attend art classes at the Art Institute of Chicago, where she studied under John Vanderpoel, whose lectures of the human figure were later printed as *The Human Figure*. After a month in Chicago, Georgia was ranked fourth out of the class of forty-four students, and by February of the following year, first. At the end of the year she returned to Williamsburg and suffered a bout of typhoid fever. During her long recovery she continued to paint, setting up an easel in the yard.

In 1907 she went to New York to the Art Students League, the alma mater of her principal and mentor at Chatham. Here she studied portraits and still lifes with William Merritt Chase, and anatomy with Kenyon Cox. Students at the League frequently asked one another to pose. A student named Eugene Speicher stopped Georgia, who was on her way to class, on the stairs one morning with that request. When she declined, he said, ''It doesn't matter what you do. I'm going to be a great painter and you will probably end up teaching painting in some girls' school.'' She returned to pose for him when she found that the model for the art class she was hurrying to was a man she disliked. Eugene Speicher's portrait, which still hangs at the Art Students League, is a charming, but standard piece of work. Its main interest is the subject: Georgia O'Keeffe.

It was the day after she posed for Speicher that O'Keeffe and a number of students went down to see a series of sketches by the great French sculptor Auguste Rodin at 291 Fifth Avenue. This gallery was owned and run by Alfred Stieglitz who by then had developed a reputation as a photographer and as a champion of new artists. O'Keeffe's recollection of their meeting had more to do with her dislike of the Rodin sketches than with the man who was showing them.

At the end of the year O'Keeffe won Chase's still life prize for a painting of a rabbit lying beside a copper pot. The prize was $100 and a place at the Art Students League summer school on Lake George. Technically O'Keeffe was becoming a very proficient artist, but what she painted for her instructors did not give her the satisfaction of the work she did for herself.

While her schooling and painting were going well, life for the rest of the O'Keeffe family was becoming difficult. Francis O'Keeffe's grocery store and feed business in Williamsburg had failed and the family was having financial difficulties. To help her family Georgia went to Chicago and took a job as a free-lance illustrator drawing lace patterns and advertisements, one of the few remunerative ways she knew of using her art training. This came to an end when she caught

measles, which temporarily weakened her eyes, and Georgia had to go back to Williamsburg. Further sadness awaited her there. Her mother had been diagnosed with tuberculosis, the disease which had killed two of Georgia's uncles. There was no known cure at that time, but mountain air was considered healthier, so Georgia and her mother moved to Charlottesville, near the foot of the Blue Ridge Mountains.

That summer Georgia studied with Alon Bement at the University of Virginia. Bement was known for his experimentation with non-representational shapes and patterns, which forced his students to learn basic concepts of balance and composition. In the fall Georgia found a position as the art supervisor of public schools in Amarillo, Texas. O'Keeffe was immediately taken by the stark beauty of the Southwest. ''That was my country,'' she later wrote, ''terrible winds and wonderful emptiness.'' The job was less successful. O'Keeffe disagreed with the school board over the use of an approved text. She thought it would be easier for the students to draw objects they were familiar with, and even permitted a boy to bring his pony into the classroom as a model. Her individuality also irritated the school board.

During the summer of 1913 she returned to Charlottesville for summer school at the University, but now she

Opposite top left:
O'Keeffe's *Portrait of Claudia,* painted in 1905.

Opposite top right:
O'Keeffe's *My Auntie*, ink on paper, 1905.

Right:
William Merritt Chase with students at Shinnecock Hills, c. 1901. O'Keeffe attended Chase's still life class and won the Chase Scholarship and a chance for further study.

O'Keeffe's watercolor
Seated Nude X
was painted in 1917.
She painted few nudes in her lifetime.

was an art instructor, assisting Bement. He continued to critique her work, and that summer introduced her to the theories of the Russian painter Wassily Kandinsky, who saw a connection between the visual arts and music and was also interested in the psychological effects of color. Bement suggested that she attend Columbia Teachers College and study with Arthur Dow, who was influenced by abstraction and Oriental concepts of art and shape. Studying with Dow, O'Keeffe's dwindling interest in her own painting revived. He taught her "the importance of design of filling space in a beautiful way." It was while she was at Columbia that she met Anita Pollitzer, another student who would become her lifelong friend. Together they explored New York and the art world, including many trips to Stieglitz's gallery, 291.

In the fall of 1915 O'Keeffe accepted a teaching position in South Carolina, which was closer to her family and her mother whose health was continuing to weaken. She wrote often to Anita Pollitzer, discussing art and life. The general unhappiness of her life pervaded their letters, but in her solitude O'Keeffe was working, drawing with charcoal in a way that no one had taught her, but which she found satisfactory. "One day, I found myself saying to myself, 'I can't live where I want to. I can't even say what I want to.' I decided I was a very stupid fool not to at least paint as I want to."

Eventually she sent a roll of these sketches and watercolors to Pollitzer, but asked her not to show them to anyone else. Later Pollitzer wrote, "I was struck by their aliveness. They were different. Here were charcoals — on the same kind of paper that all art students were using, and through no trick, no superiority of tools, these drawings were saying something that had not yet been said."

Pollitzer felt that it was extremely important for someone else, someone who was part of the art world, to see O'Keeffe's new work, and she and O'Keeffe had written to one another and discussed the many exhibits that they had seen at 291. So Pollitzer took the sketches to Alfred Stieglitz. Apparently she said nothing to him about the artist, and Stieglitz, who was always interested in new talent, looked through them very carefully. "Finally," he said, "a woman on paper."

Pollitzer's letter to O'Keeffe confessing that she had in fact shown the sketches, also quotes Stieglitz, who said, "they're the purest, finest, sincerest things that have entered 291 in a long while . . . I wouldn't mind showing them in one of these rooms one bit." O'Keeffe wrote to Pollitzer to thank her, and also to Stieglitz asking him to tell her about his feelings for her work. He did in a most encouraging manner.

At the same time that her artistic career was beginning to flower O'Keeffe once again changed positions, taking a new post as head of the art department at West Texas State Normal College in Canyon, a town about twenty miles south of Amarillo. This adjustment meant another teaching course in New York. It was during this time, in late spring of 1916, that O'Keeffe discovered that Stieglitz had included her sketches in a small exhibition without her permission. But when she arrived at gallery, feeling angry and betrayed, Stieglitz was away for the

Alfred Stieglitz
at his gallery "291" in 1915.

day. The gallery was empty of people and O'Keeffe had the opportunity to study her drawings privately. The following day she returned, still ready to insist on the return of her property. Stieglitz persuaded her to leave them, questioning her about her ideas and how she executed them. Like many other artists, O'Keeffe found it impossible to resist Stieglitz's interest and passion for art.

In September, O'Keeffe went back to Texas, and again was inspired by the landscape. She began a series of watercolors, including the now-famous "Blue" watercolors. She continued to write to Stieglitz, and in April of 1917, she had her first solo show at 291. The review in the *Christian Science Monitor* is somewhat prophetic. "Her strange art affects people variously and some not at all . . . artists especially wonder at its technical resourcefulness for dealing with what hitherto has been deemed the inexpressible." The same sentiment might be descriptive of all her works.

These grotesque formations stand watch over the
colorful, wild country north of Santa Fe. This is the type
of rugged land O'Keeffe often painted.

When O'Keeffe was at last free to return to New York,
the show was over, but Stieglitz kindly rehung it for her. He also
took pictures of her with her work, in his usual manner,
focusing on a single part of the artist, frequently her expressive
hands. It was something he only did to someone to whom he
felt close.

O'Keeffe returned to Texas with her youngest sister
Claudia who was now living with her following the death of
their mother the preceding May. That summer the two
O'Keeffes went west, to Colorado, which Georgia described in a
letter to photographer Paul Strand, ''The mountains like silver in
the moonlight – The black into the pines and into the valleys
seemed impossibly black.''

Another stop was Santa Fe, New Mexico, which
O'Keeffe fell in love with. ''From then on,'' she later wrote, ''I
was always trying to get back.''

She returned to Canyon for another year of teaching.

The United States had been swept by war fever at this point,
some six months after the entry into World War I. O'Keeffe
stood apart from the rest of the faculty and students at the
college for she was a pacifist. The strain of the past few years
was beginning to show. In January 1918, like many thousands of
other Americans, O'Keeffe came down with influenza. She was
granted a leave of absence but her recuperation was very slow.
Eventually, Stieglitz sent Paul Strand down to Texas to bring her
back to New York.

The relationship of Stieglitz and O'Keeffe, which had
begun with exchanges of letters about art and life, had grown
in affection. It was probably at this time, while O'Keeffe was
practically confined to the small studio on 59th Street, that they
became lovers. Despite their differences in age (Stieglitz was
fifty-five, O'Keeffe was thirty), their convictions about many
things drew them together. Stieglitz's marriage had been
unhappy for many years, but the acceptance of the irregular

relationship between O'Keeffe and Stieglitz by the Stieglitz family was remarkable for 1918.

O'Keeffe's new position gave her among other things, the time and independence to paint, and Stieglitz encouraged her to develop new styles using different mediums. Stieglitz continued to take photographs of her, and began a major series of them in 1919. In 1921 the Anderson Galleries held a retrospective exhibition of Stieglitz's photographs. Out of 145 photos selected, 45 were pictures of O'Keeffe.

Joining the Stieglitz family meant that O'Keeffe became part of the extended group who traveled to Lake George in upstate New York every summer. This brought O'Keeffe back to an area she had enjoyed and painted when a student. She also discovered the beauty of coastal Maine, and began to take annual trips to York Beach. She rarely painted landscapes there but would paint still lifes which became abstractions, finding beauty in shells juxtaposed with weather-worn shingles.

In 1923 O'Keeffe held her first one-woman show in six years at the Anderson Galleries. Titled ''One Hundred Pictures,'' all the works were unsigned for O'Keeffe had decided her signature was not part of the paintings. The following year she began to work on the massive flower paintings which may be her best known work. Many of these are close-ups of blossoms, which seem to focus on the heart of each flower. The paintings are not detailed, but painted in clear colors, with subtle tones and shades. In that era, which had recently become aware of

O'Keeffe's *Red Barn*, painted
while in Lake George, New York, in 1921.

13

Freud and his theories, many critics found sexual symbolism in these paintings, but that had not been O'Keeffe's purpose.

In September of 1922 Stieglitz was finally divorced from his wife, but it was not until December of 1924 that he persuaded O'Keeffe to marry him, in a civil ceremony on December 11. She was thirty-seven, he was sixty-one. Despite their respect and love for one another, their marriage was not perfect. Stieglitz was gregarious, delighting in the intellectual arguments that seemed to follow him. O'Keeffe, on the other hand, treasured solitude and could not work when there was any distraction. She made herself a studio out of an old shack up at Lake George, and no one else was allowed in it.

In 1925 she and Stieglitz moved into an apartment on the thirtieth floor of the Hotel Shelton, one of the first residential skyscrapers. The view gave O'Keeffe a different perspective on the city, and she painted a series of paintings which capture the vibrancy of New York. Many of these were done at night, showing the new towers lit with neon.

O'Keeffe's public reputation was further enhanced by the purchase of a series of six calla lily paintings by a French collector for the incredible sum of $25,000 in 1928. The purchase made headlines in the New York papers, and people became interested in the artist who seemed to paint like no one else in the world. Later that year, after a trip to Wisconsin to visit relatives, O'Keeffe returned to New York just before Stieglitz suffered his first heart attack. This intimation of mortality changed Stieglitz. He became even more set in his ways, while O'Keeffe was still interested in traveling to new and different places. Though he became more dependent upon her at a time when she required a great deal of solitude, their affection remained strong and his interest in her work continued.

The following April, O'Keeffe and Rebecca Strand, the wife of Paul Strand, who was known as ''Beck,'' went out to New Mexico, and encountered Mabel Dodge Luhan, an extraordinary art patron, who had married a Pueblo Indian. Luhan offered O'Keeffe a studio for the summer, and the artist, delighted to be in the Southwest again, began to paint the starkly beautiful landscape around Taos. She bought a small Ford and learned to drive so that she could be more independent and explore the desert. She began to paint the heavy adobe churches and the dark crosses of the Penitente, which were to be found in the more remote parts of the state.

When she returned to Stieglitz in August, she was happy to go up to Lake George to finish a few paintings, and to begin others, while Stieglitz made plans for the opening of his new gallery, An American Place. Before the first exhibition opened, however, New York experienced the stock market crash in October. That same year O'Keeffe was asked to include a number of paintings in the first exhibitions held by the newly founded Museum of Modern Art.

O'Keeffe continued to travel out to New Mexico each year and began to paint the stark bones that are found in the desert. Rather than use them as part of a still life, she combined them abstractly with artificial flowers or landscapes. When they were first exhibited in 1932, they baffled the critics.

In April, O'Keeffe had accepted, against Stieglitz's wishes, a commission to decorate one of the ladies' lounges in Radio City Music Hall, which was nearing completion. Unfortunately, there were technical difficulties preparing the room. Before it was ready, O'Keeffe suffered a nervous

breakdown, and the commission was given to another artist.

O'Keeffe sold her first painting, *Black Flower and Blue Larkspur*, to the Metropolitan Museum of Art in 1934. It was proof of her standing in the art world, and of the sudden interest of the major museums in modern art. O'Keeffe continued to exhibit, and to spend a few months of each year in New Mexico. The exhibitions included a joint one with John Marin, Arthur Dove, Charles Demuth and Marsden Hartley, four other painters whose careers Stieglitz had encouraged and who had influenced one another.

In 1936 O'Keeffe accepted a commission from Elizabeth Arden, the great entrepreneur of beauty products, to paint one of her massive flower paintings. The final work, *White Jimson Blossoms,* for which the artist received $10,000, still hangs in the entrance hall at Elizabeth Arden's Maine Chance spa in Phoenix, Arizona. At this time she also designed a lily pattern to be engraved on crystal bowls for the Steuben Glass Company. In 1938 the Dole Pineapple Company invited her to go to Hawaii to paint their symbol. She found it difficult to come to grips with the project, although she painted a beautiful red ginger flower and a papaya tree. In the end, Dole had to be content with a pineapple bud, but the image appeared on their advertising for years.

O'Keeffe was also honored by several colleges and universities. The College of William and Mary in Williamsburg, Virginia, gave her an Honorary Doctorate of Fine Arts. Ironically,

it had been the college that her brother Francis attended, which at that time, O'Keeffe could not have attended, for it was an all-male institution.

The seasons spent in New Mexico continued to revive O'Keeffe. In 1940, she bought her first piece of property, the mysterious and remote Ghost Ranch. Five years later she bought an ancient abandoned house near the village of Abiquiu and began the extensive restoration project that would take three years.

In 1939 O'Keeffe was selected as one of the twelve most outstanding women of the past fifty years by the New York World's Fair Tomorrow Committee. Her painting *Sunset, Long Island* was chosen to represent New York State in an exhibition of the art of the United States at the World's Fair.

The great difference in age between Stieglitz and O'Keeffe became more and more divisive. The stamina required to satisfy the whims of an aging man continued to deplete her of what she required to complete her works. Their affection, despite a few affairs on his part and despite O'Keeffe's continuing trips to New Mexico, had remained strong. She was in New Mexico when she received word in July 1946 that Stieglitz had suffered a stroke. Without stopping to pack she returned to New York, and was beside him when he died on July 13, 1946. He was eighty-two.

Stieglitz's will named O'Keeffe principal heir and executrix. For the next three years she spent time organizing and disposing of Stieglitz's art collection, which consisted of over 850 works of art and thousands of photographs. The bulk of this was given to the Metropolitan Museum of Art, following two retrospective exhibitions, one of the collection and one of Stieglitz's own photographs. A prodigious correspondent, Stieglitz also left some 50,000 letters. O'Keeffe wrote to many of his old friends requesting other letters, so that the file would be complete. A master set of Stieglitz photographs was also given to the National Gallery. With this accomplished, O'Keeffe moved out to New Mexico and the newly restored house at Abiquiu.

One year later, she closed down Stieglitz's gallery, An American Place, when the building was slated for demolition. The final exhibition there was one of her own.

She continued to paint, working especially on two series, *The Black Place,* a series of landscapes of the cleft in the hills, and the paintings that featured the great framing shapes of the cattle pelvises O'Keeffe collected in the desert. She became something of a recluse from the art world, although she continued to travel and continued to receive awards and honorary degrees. The trend in art had turned to abstract expressionism, but O'Keeffe continued to paint in her own idiosyncratic style.

In 1960 she held her first major exhibition since 1946, that last one Stieglitz had arranged at An American Place, at the Worcester Art Museum, in Worcester, Massachusetts. A new generation was stunned and confused by her work, asking the same questions, and occasionally coming to the same incorrect conclusions that critics had in the twenties.

Many of her later works were inspired by the views of

Above:
O'Keeffe's *Near Abiquiu, New Mexico,* painted in 1930.

Right:
O'Keeffe was inspired by the many adobe churches and buildings of New Mexico. This adobe church was erected at Ranchos de Taos, circa 1776.

the earth she saw when she traveled by plane. These included the series called *From the River* and *Sky Above Clouds*. One of the latter, *IV,* was the largest painting she ever worked on, and measured a full 24-by-8-feet. The only building large enough to hold the canvas was her garage, and O'Keeffe had to build a short scaffolding so that she could paint the top of the canvas. The bottom of it she painted sitting on the ground. She was then seventy-eight.

Another retrospective in 1970, arranged by the Whitney Museum of Art in New York, introduced O'Keeffe to yet another generation. Some found her work surprisingly derivative of younger painters, not realizing that she had come first. The great art critic, John Canaday delighted in pointing this out. "Strolling through the show, one could think that Miss O'Keeffe has made some very neat adaptations of various successful styles of the 1950s and 1960s in her own highly refined and slightly removed manner." He found apparent similarities to the works of such artists as Helen Frankenthaler, Barnett Newman, Ad Reinhardt and Andrew Wyeth. But those painters "were either not yet born or delighting their mothers with their first childish scrawls" when O'Keeffe had painted the works that some seemed to find too similar.

O'Keeffe was now eighty-two, and though she seemed as physically healthy as ever, she was growing old. The following year her eyesight began to fail. She lost her central vision, retaining only her peripheral vision, and was forced to stop painting. She became more and more reclusive, resenting some of the people who sometimes traveled for miles hoping to see her. In 1976 she published her autobiography, which gave some insight into her paintings, but very little into her own life. To celebrate her ninetieth birthday, National Educational Television commissioned a biography. And in 1978 she worked on the catalogue and exhibition of photographs entitled *Georgia O'Keeffe: A Portrait by Alfred Stieglitz.* She continued to travel although it became more and more difficult. Finally friends made her move to Santa Fe to be closer to any necessary medical attention. Georgia O'Keeffe died on March 6, 1986, in her ninety-ninth year. In her last year of life she had been granted the Medal of Arts by President Reagan, and the years following her death saw further exhibitions and the publication of numerous books including *One Hundred Flowers* and *Georgia O'Keeffe: Art and Letters.* Many of her paintings have become almost too familiar, but closer examination brings the viewer back to the state of finding something rich and strange.

In 1926 the writer Blanche Matthias, who later became a close friend, wrote about the exhibition at the Intimate Gallery: "She is like the flickering flame of a candle, steady, serene, softly brilliant . . . This woman who lives fearlessly, reasons logically, who is modest, unassertive and spiritually beautiful and who, because she dares to paint as she feels, has become not only one of the most magical artists of our time but one of the most stimulatingly powerful." Nothing that O'Keeffe painted in the following sixty years would have made Matthias change her mind.

One of America's most original artists –
Georgia O'Keeffe in 1970 at the age of 83.

The Plates

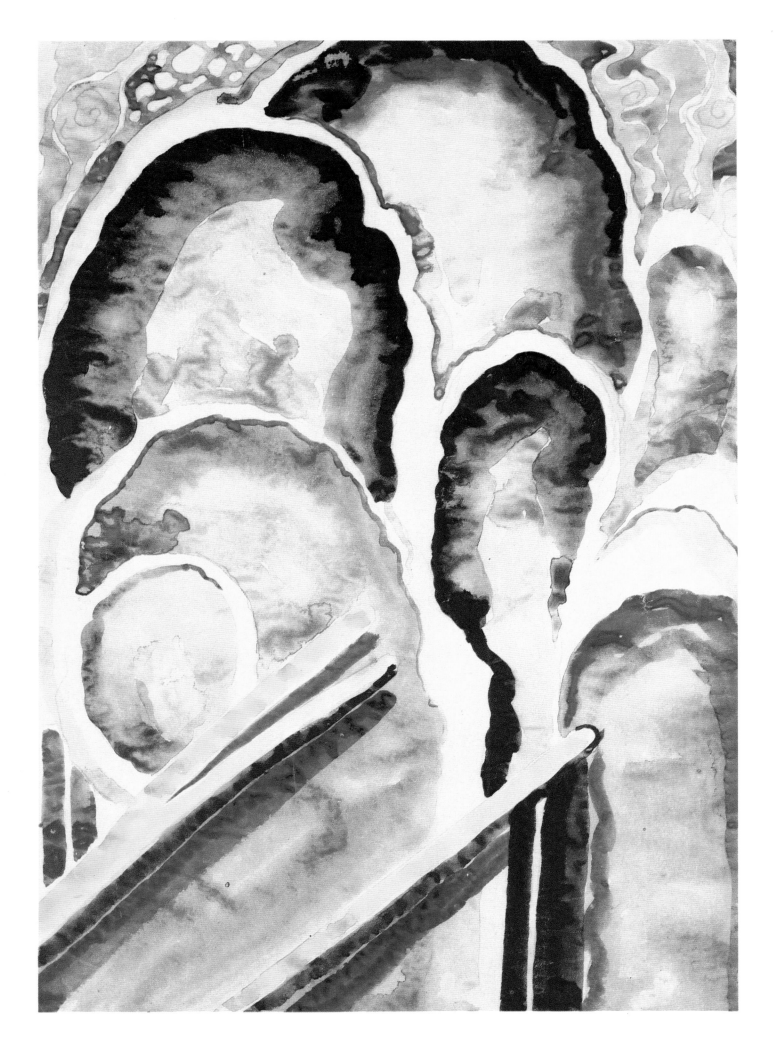

Left:

Red Canna

c. 1920, watercolor on paper, 19⅜ × 13 in.

*Gift of George Hooper Fitch, B.A. 1932,
and Mrs. Fitch, Yale University Art Gallery,
New Haven, CT*

Right:

Pansy

1926, oil on canvas, 26¹⁵⁄₁₆ × 12¹⁄₁₆ in.

*Gift of Mrs. Alfred S. Rossin,
The Brooklyn Museum, Brooklyn, NY
(28.521)*

Overleaf:

Oriental Poppies

1928, oil on canvas, 30 × 40⅛ in.

*University Art Museum,
University of Minnesota, Minneapolis, MN
(37.1)*

Left:

Large Dark Red Leaves on White

1925, oil on canvas, 32 × 21 in.

*Acquired 1943, The Phillips Collection,
Washington, D.C.*

Above:

Pattern of Leaves

c. 1923, oil on canvas, 22⅛ × 18⅛ in.

*Acquired 1926, The Phillips Collection,
Washington, D.C.*

Above:
Purple Leaves
1922, oil on canvas on board, 12 × 9 in.

Bequest of Virginia Rike Haswell,
Dayton Institute of Art, Dayton, OH
(77.60)

Right:
Oak Leaves – Pink and Gray
1929, oil on canvas, 33⅛ × 18 in.

General Budget Fund, 1936,
University Gallery, University of Minnesota,
Minneapolis, MN
(36.85)

Page 34:
Light Iris
1924, oil on canvas, 40 × 30 in.

Gift of Mr. and Mrs. Bruce C. Gottwald
Virginia Museum of Fine Arts, Richmond, VA
(85.1534)

Page 35:
Grey Line with Black, Blue and Yellow
c. 1923, oil on canvas, 48 × 30 in.

Museum purchase with funds provided by the
Agnes Cullen Arnold Endowment Fund,
The Museum of Fine Arts, Houston, TX

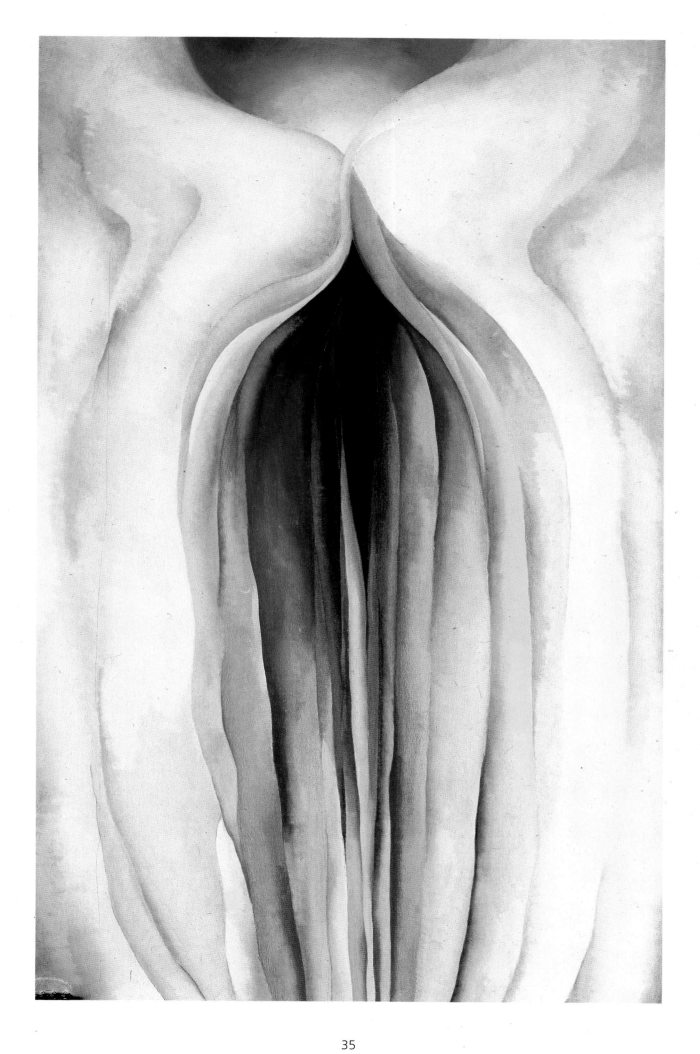

Above:

Purple Petunias

1925, oil on canvas, 15⅞ × 13 in.

Bequest of Miss Cora Louise Hartshorn, 1958,
Collection of The Newark Museum, Newark, NJ
(58.167)

Right:

Calla Lilly on Grey

1928, oil on canvas, 32 × 17 in.

Gift of the William H. Lane Foundation,
Courtesy of Museum of Fine Arts, Boston
(1990.431)

Above:

Black Iris III

1926, oil on canvas, 36 × 29⅞ in.

Alfred Stieglitz Collection, 1969,
The Metropolitan Museum of Art, New York, NY
(69.278.1)

Right:

Iris

1929, oil on canvas, 32 × 12 in.

Anonymous gift,
Colorado Springs Fine Arts Center,
Colorado Springs, CO

Pink Roses and Larkspur

1931, pastel on paper, 16 × 12 in.

Museum of Western Art, Denver, CO
(7.87)

Above:

Squash Flowers No. 1

1925, oil on cardboard, 13¾ × 18¹⁄₁₆ in.

Gift of Mr. and Mrs. Allan D. Emil, 1955,
Smith College Museum of Art, Northampton, MA
(1955:46)

Top left:
White Flower
1929, oil on canvas, 30⅛ × 36⅛ in.

The Hinman B. Hurlbut Collection,
The Cleveland Museum of Art, Cleveland, OH
(2162.30)

Bottom left:
Morning Glory with Black
c. 1926, oil on canvas, 35¹³⁄₁₆ × 39⅝ in.

Bequest of Leonard C. Hanna, Jr.,
The Cleveland Museum of Art, Cleveland, OH
(58.42)

Above:
White Trumpet Flower
1932, oil on canvas, 29¾ × 39¾ in.

Gift of Mrs. Inez Grant Parker in memory of
Earle W. Grant, San Diego Museum of Art, San Diego, CA
(1971:012)

Narcissa's Last Orchid
1941, pastel, 21⅜ × 27⅛ in.

Gift of David H. McAlpin,
The Art Museum, Princeton University, Princeton, NJ

Datura and Pedernal

1940, oil on canvas, 11 × 16⅛ in.

Gift of Dorothy Meigs Eidlitz Foundation, 1969,
Orlando Museum of Art, Orlando, FL
(69.1.1)

Yellow Hickory Leaves with Daisy

1928, oil on canvas, 29¾ × 39¾ in.

Gift of Georgia O'Keeffe to the
Alfred Stieglitz Collection, 1965,
The Art Institute of Chicago, Chicago, IL

Black Hollyhock, Blue Larkspur
1929, oil on canvas, 36 × 30 in.

George A. Hearn Fund, 1934,
The Metropolitan Museum of Art, New York, NY
(34.51)

Above:

Jimsonweed

1936, oil on canvas, 70 × 83½ in.

On loan from Eli Lilly & Company,
Indianapolis Museum of Art, Indianapolis, IN
(TR 6623)

Right:

Blue and Green Music

1919, oil on canvas, 23 × 19 in.

Gift of Georgia O'Keeffe to the Alfred Stieglitz Collection,
The Art Institute of Chicago
Chicago, IL

Left:

Corn Dark, I

1924, oil on composition board, 31¾ × 11⅞ in.

The Alfred Stieglitz Collection, 1950,
The Metropolitan Museum of Art, New York, NY
(50.236.1)

Above:

Spring (detail)

1922, oil on canvas, 35½ × 30⅜ in.

Bequest of Mrs. Arthur Schwab (Edna Bryner '07)
Vassar College Art Gallery, Poughkeepsie, NY
(67.31.15)

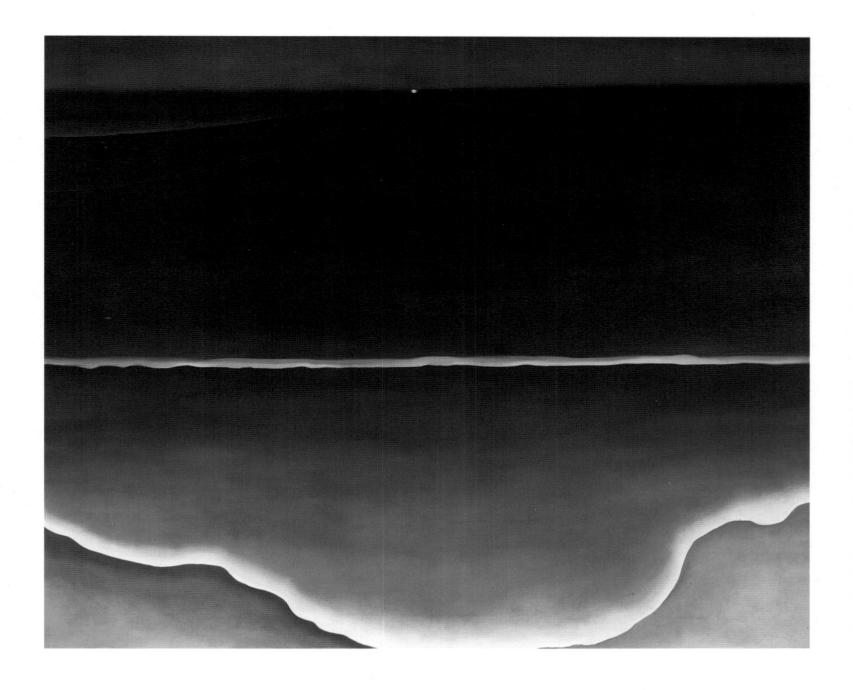

Above:

The Lawrence Tree

1929, oil on canvas, 31¹⁄₁₆ × 39³⁄₁₆ in.

*Ella Gallup Sumner and Mary Catlin Sumner Collection,
Courtesy of the Estate of Georgia O'Keeffe,
Wadsworth Atheneum, Hartford, CT*

Right:

Birch Trees at Dawn on Lake George

1926, oil on canvas, 36 × 30 in.

*Gift of Mrs. Ernest W. Stix,
The Saint Louis Art Museum,
St. Louis, MO
(14.1964)*

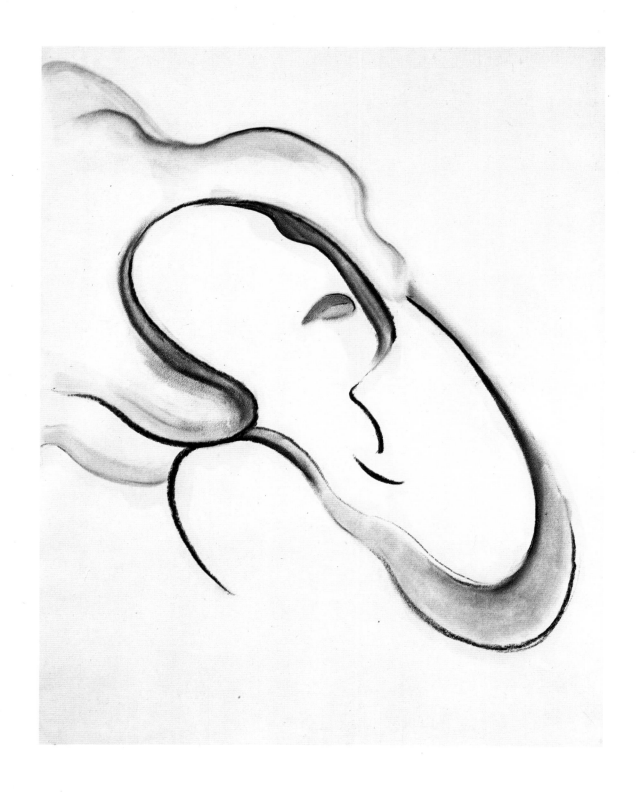

Above:

Abstraction IX

1916, charcoal on paper, 24¼ × 18¾ in.

Alfred Stieglitz Collection, 1969,
The Metropolitan Museum of Art, New York, NY
(69.278.4)

Right:

Blue Lines X

1916, watercolor on paper, 25 × 19 in.

Alfred Stieglitz Collection, 1969,
The Metropolitan Museum of Art, New York, NY
(69.278.3)

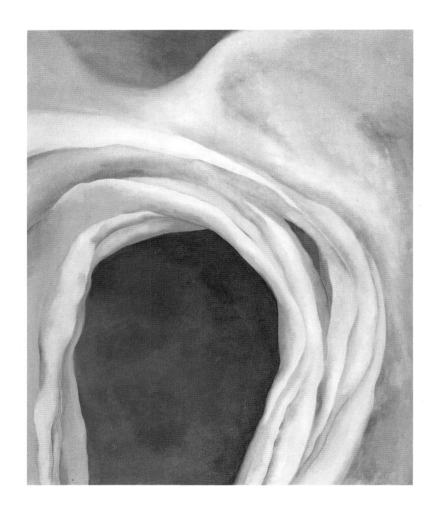

Below:

East River No. 1

1926, oil on linen, 12⅛ × 32⅛ in.

*Gift of the Museum Shop Volunteers,
Wichita Art Museum, Wichita, KS
(1979.35)*

Right:

Shell and Shingle VI

1926, oil on canvas, 30¹⁄₁₆ × 17⅞ in.

*Gift of Charles E. Claggett in memory of
Blanche Fischel Claggett,
The Saint Louis Art Museum, St. Louis, MO*

Overleaf:

A Storm

1922, pastel on paper, 18¼ × 24⅜ in.

*Anonymous gift, 1981,
The Metropolitan Museum of Art, New York, NY
(1981.35)*

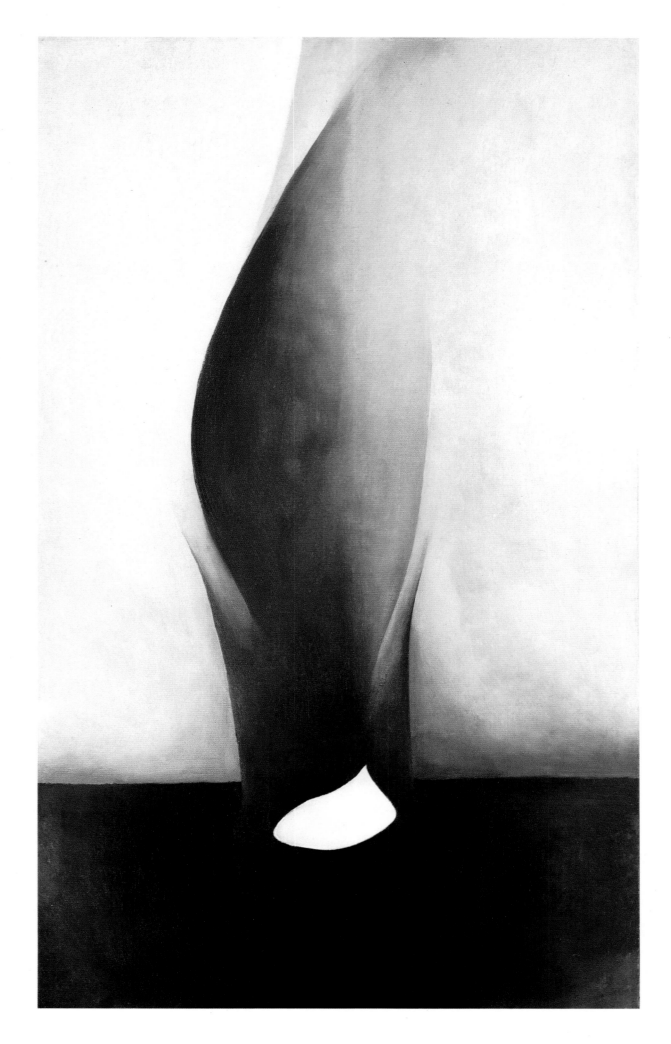

Black, White, and Blue
1930, oil on canvas, 48 × 30 in.
Collection of Barney A. Ebsworth

Black Place II

1944, oil on canvas, 23⅛ × 30 in.

Alfred Stieglitz Collection, 1959,
The Metropolitan Museum of Art, New York, NY
(59.204.1)

Left:

White Abstraction (Madison Avenue)

1926, oil on canvas, 32½ × 12 in.

*Gift of Charles C. and Margaret Stevenson Henderson
in memory of Hunt Henderson,
Collection of Museum of Fine Arts, St. Petersburg, FL*

Above:

Lake George, New York

c. 1927, oil on canvas, 8¾ × 15¾ in.

*Rebecca Salsbury James Collection, 1968,
Museum of Fine Arts, Museum of New Mexico,
Santa Fe, NM
(2287.23P)*

73

Left:

Brown Sail, Wing and Wing, Nassau

1940, oil on canvas, 38 × 30¹⁄₁₆ in.

Museum Purchase Fund, Toledo Museum of Art,
Toledo, OH
(1949.106)

Above:

Tent Door at Night

c.1913, watercolor on paper, 19 × 24¾ in.

Purchased through the Julius Rolshoven Memorial Fund
with the assistance of the Friends of Art,
University of New Mexico Art Museum
Albuquerque, New Mexico
(72.157)

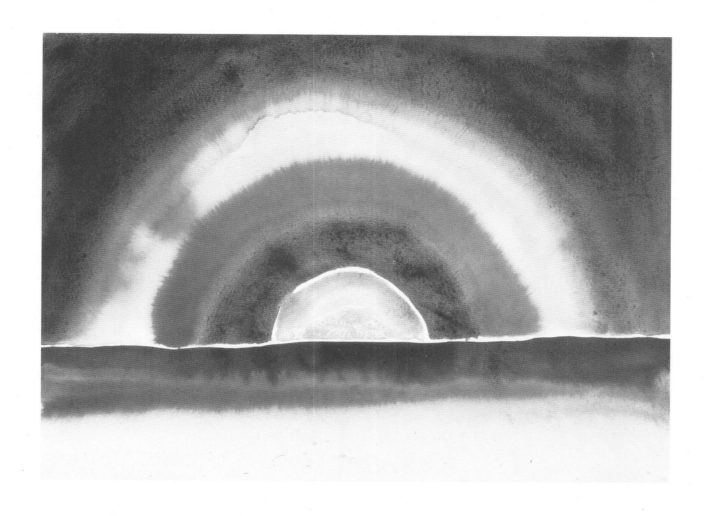

Left:

Seated Nude XI

1917, watercolor on paper, 11⅞ × 8⅞ in.

Purchase, Mr. and Mrs. Milton Petrie Gift, 1981
The Metropolitan Museum of Art, New York, NY
(1981.194)

Above:

Sunrise

1917, watercolor, 8⅞ × 11⅞ in.

Collection of Barney A. Ebsworth

Overleaf:

Black Abstraction

1927, oil on canvas, 30 × 40¼ in.

Alfred Stieglitz Collection,
The Metropolitan Museum of Art, New York, NY

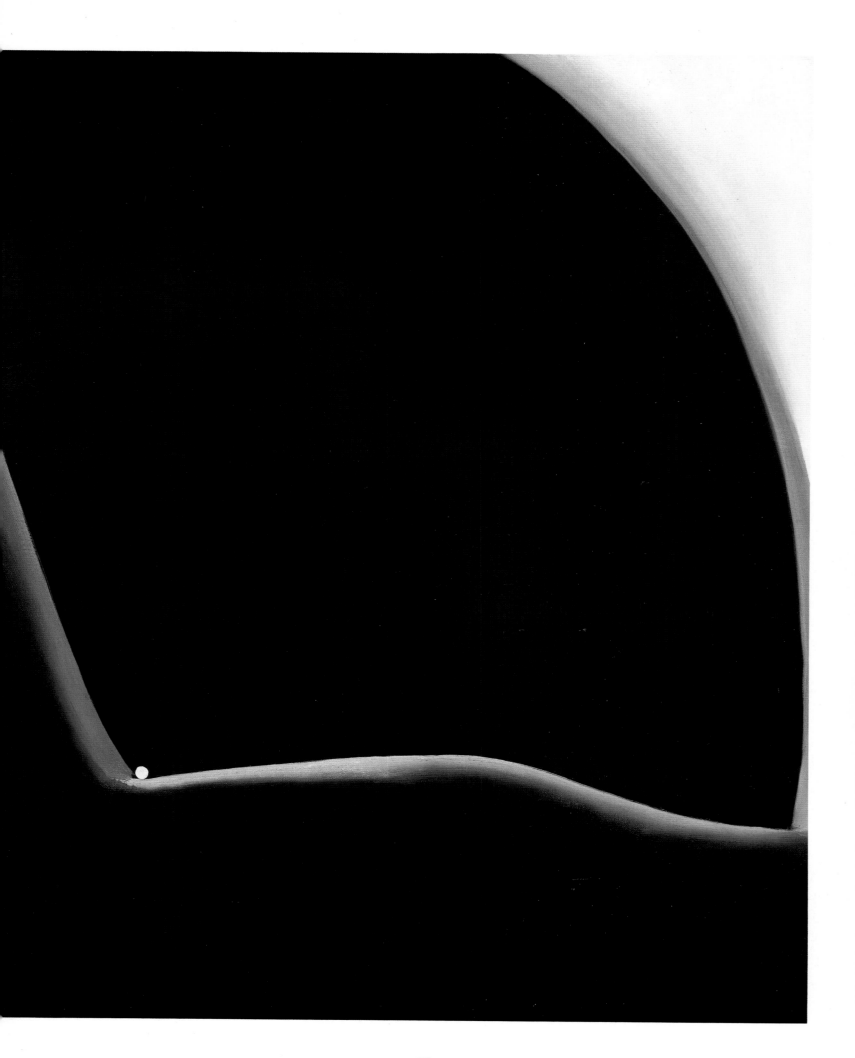

Gray Tree by the Road
1952, oil on canvas, 15$\frac{15}{16}$ × 20$\frac{1}{16}$ in.

Gift of Mrs. Bernhard G. Bechhoefer
In the Collection of The Corcoran Gallery of Art, Washington, D.C.
(1984.20)

Horn and Feather
1937, oil on canvas, 9 × 14 in.
Collection of Barney A. Ebsworth

Clam Shell
1930, oil on canvas, 24 × 36 in.
Alfred Stieglitz Collection, 1962,
The Metropolitan Museum of Art, New York, NY
(62.258)

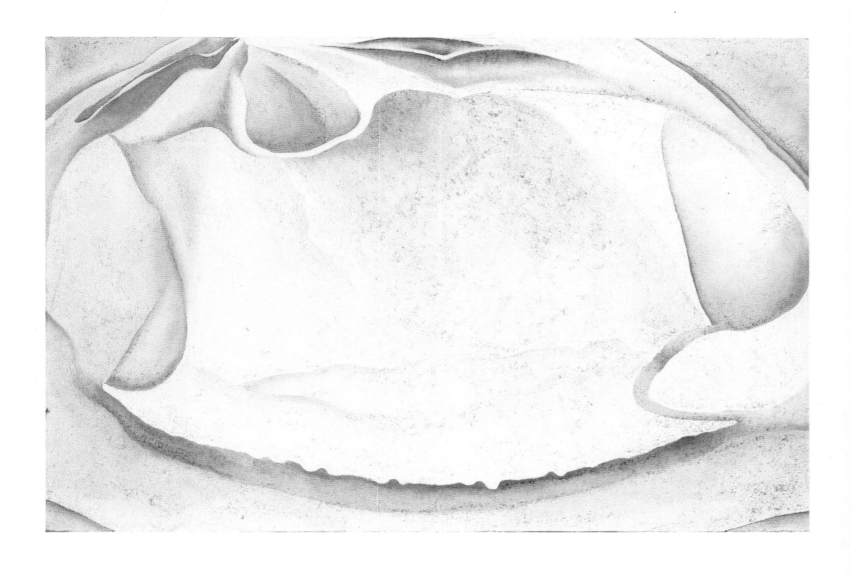

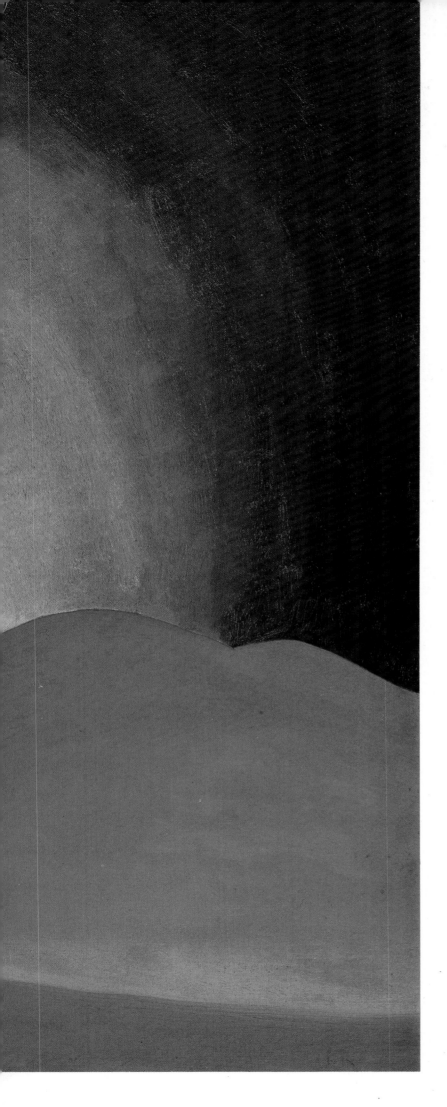

Red Hills, Lake George
1927, oil on canvas, 27 × 32 in.

Acquired 1945,
The Phillips Collection, Washington, D.C.

Katchina (detail)

1936, oil on canvas, 7 × 7 in.

Gift of the Hamilton-Wells Collection,
San Francisco Museum of Modern Art, San Francisco, CA
(76.188)

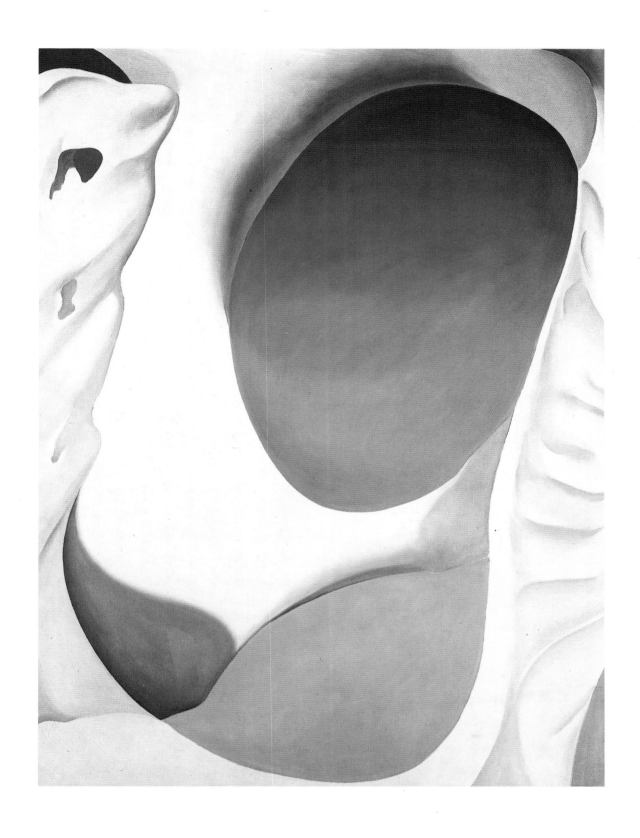

Pelvis II

1944, oil on canvas, 40 × 30 in.

George A. Hearn Fund, 1947,
The Metropolitan Museum of Art, New York, NY
(47.19)

Pelvis with Pedernal
1943, oil on canvas, 16 × 22 in.
Munson-Williams Proctor Institute of Art, Utica, NY

Stables

1932, oil on canvas, 12 × 32 in.

Gift of Robert H. Tannahill,
The Detroit Institute of Arts, MI
(45.454)

White Canadian Barn, No. 2

1932, oil on canvas, 12 × 30 in.

The Alfred Stieglitz Collection, 1964,
The Metropolitan Museum of Art, New York, NY
(64.310)

Ends of Barns

1922, oil on canvas, 16 × 22 in.

*Gift of Mr. and Mrs. William H. Lane,
Juliana Cheney Edwards Collection,
Emily L. Ainsley Fund, and Grant Walker Fund,
Courtesy of Museum of Fine Arts, Boston
(1990.380)*

Above:
My Shanty, Lake George
1922, oil on canvas, 20 × 27 in.
*Acquired 1926, The Phillips Collection,
Washington, D.C.*

Right:
Dead Cottonwood Tree, Abiquiu, New Mexico
1943, oil on canvas, 36 × 30 in.
*Gift of Mrs. Gary Cooper,
Collection of the Santa Barbara Museum of Art, Santa Barbara, CA
(1951.6)*

96

97

Cottonwood III

undated, oil on canvas, 19½ × 29¼ in.

Butler Institute of American Art, Youngstown, OH
(990.0.111))

Below:

New Mexican Landscape

1930, oil on canvas, 16 × 30 in.

The James Philip Gray Collection,
Museum of Fine Arts, Springfield, MA

Right:

Deer's Skull with Pedernal

1936, oil on canvas, 36 × 30 in.

Gift of the William H. Lane Foundation,
Courtesy of Museum of Fine Arts, Boston
(1990.432)

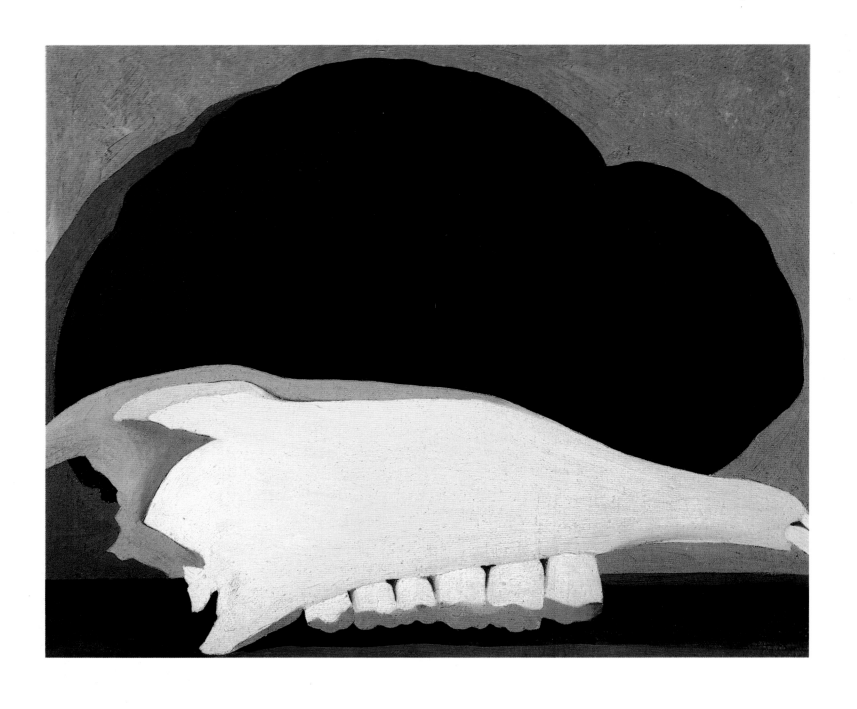

Jawbone and Fungus

1930, oil on canvas, 17 × 20 in.

Marion Stratton Gould Fund, Memorial Art Gallery
of the University of Rochester, Rochester, NY
(51.11)

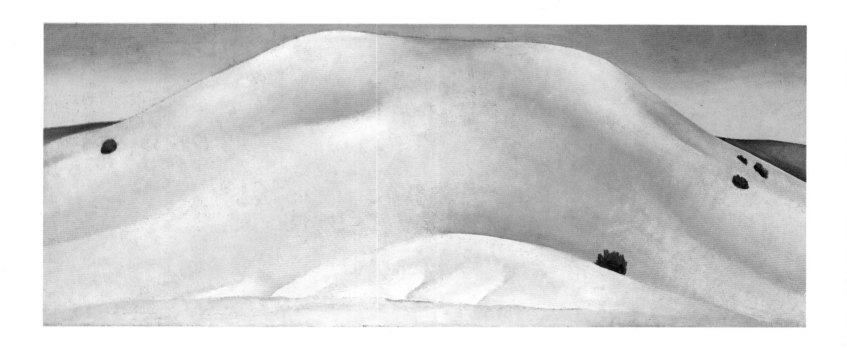

Soft Gray, Alcalde Hill (Near Alcalde, New Mexico)
1929, oil on canvas, 10⅛ × 24⅛ in.

Gift of Joseph H. Hirshhorn, 1972,
Hirshhorn Museum and Sculpture Garden,
Smithsonian Institution, Washington, D.C.
(HMSG 72.216)

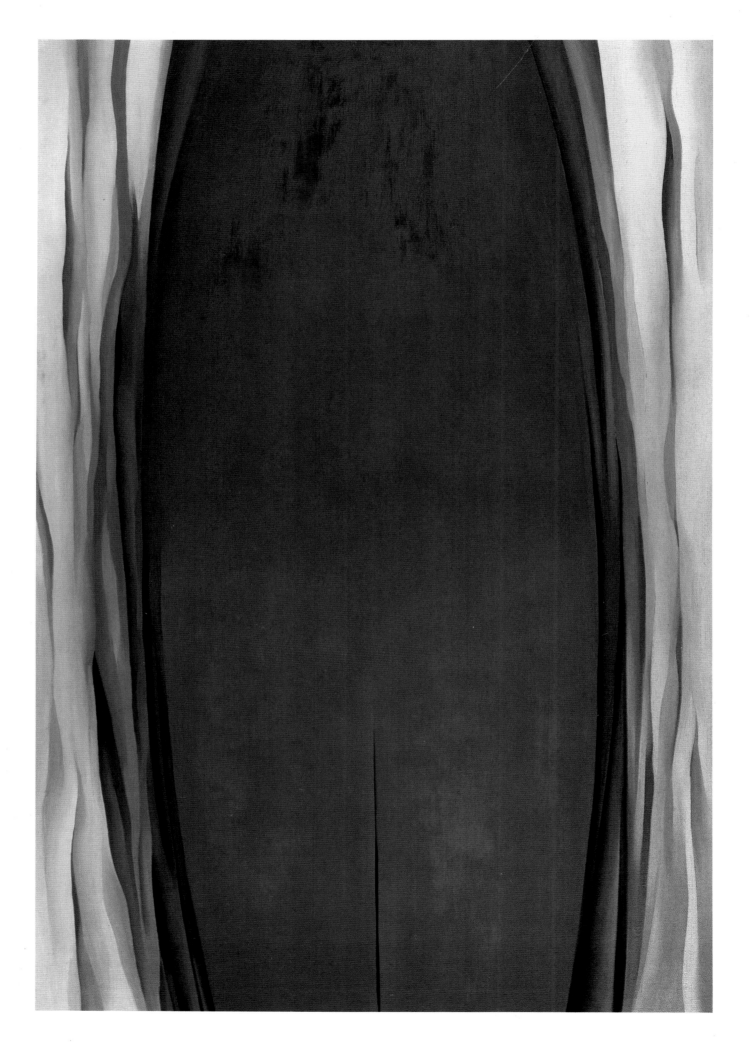

Left:

Green-Grey Abstraction

1931, oil on canvas, 36 × 24 in.

The Regis Collection, Minneapolis, MN

Above:

Abstraction – White Rose III

1927, oil on canvas, 36 × 30 in.

*Alfred Stieglitz Collection,
Bequest of Georgia O'Keeffe
The Art Institute of Chicago, Chicago, IL*

Below:

Purple Hills Near Abiquiu
1935, oil on canvas, 16⅛ × 30⅛ in.

*Gift of Mr. and Mrs. Norton S. Walbridge,
San Diego Museum of Art, San Diego, CA
(1976:216)*

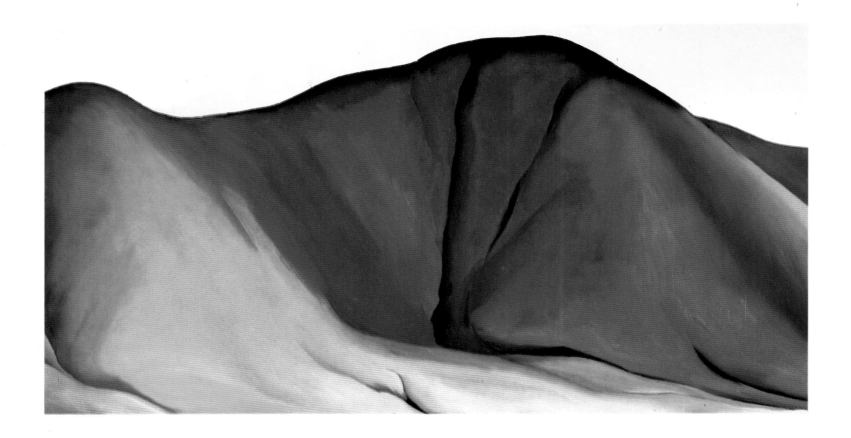

Right:

From the White Place
1940, oil on canvas, 30 × 24 in.

*Acquired 1941, The Phillips Collection,
Washington, D.C.*

Overleaf:

The Gray Hills
1942, oil on canvas, 20 × 30 in.

*Gift of Mr. and Mrs. James W. Fesler,
Indianapolis Museum of Art,
Indianapolis, IN*

Black Hills and Cedar

1942, oil on canvas, 16 × 30 in.

Gift of Joseph H. Hirshhorn,
Hirshhorn Museum and Sculpture Garden,
Smithsonian Institution, Washington, D.C.
(HMSG 86.3471)

Black Place I

1944, oil on canvas, 26 × 30⅛ in.

Gift of Charlotte Mack,
San Francisco Museum of Modern Art,
San Francisco, CA
(54.3536)

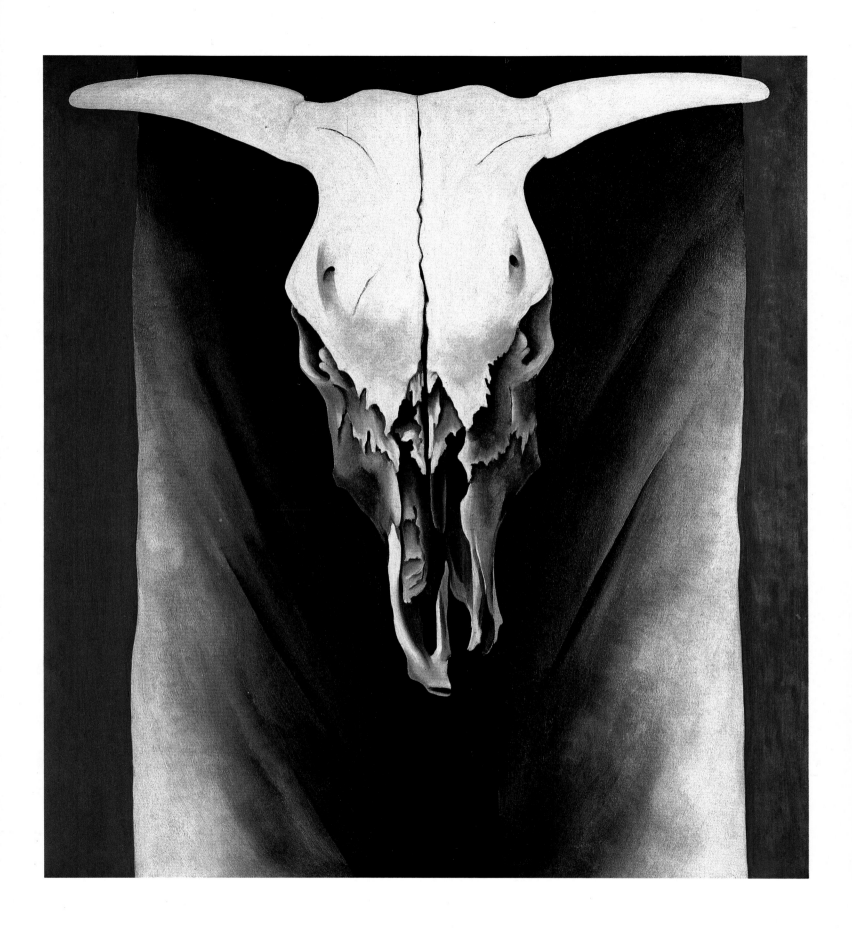

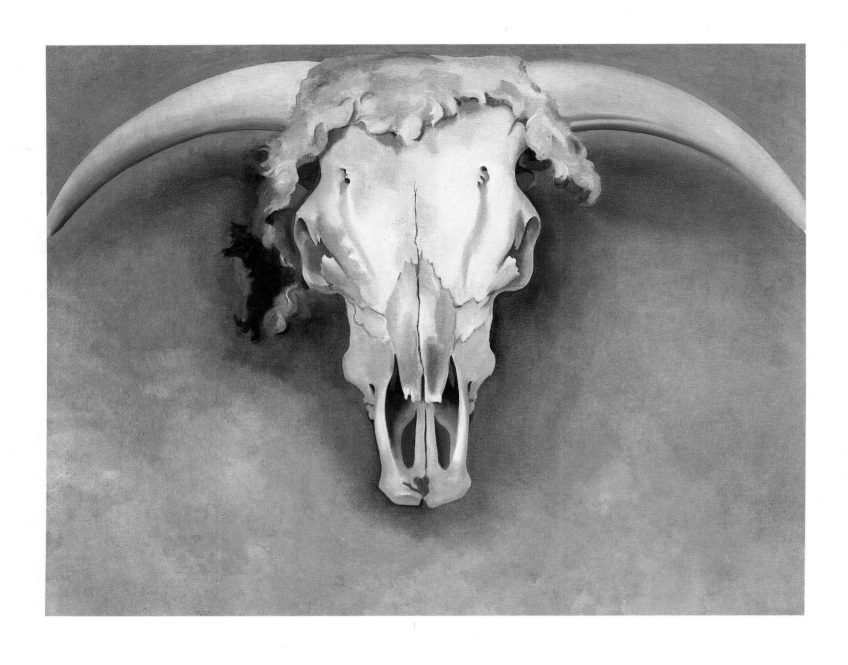

Bob's Steer Head

1936, oil on canvas, 30 × 36 in.

Gift of Arthur Milliken, B.A. 1926,
Yale University Art Gallery, New Haven, CT
(1965.52)

Ranchos Church No. 1

1929, oil on canvas, 18¾ × 24 in.

Norton Gallery of Art,
West Palm Beach, FL

Another Church, Hernandez, New Mexico
1931, oil on canvas, 10 × 24 in.
Courtesy of The Anschutz Collection

Black Cross, New Mexico

1929, oil on canvas, 39 × 30⅓ in.

*The Art Institute Purchase Fund,
The Art Institute of Chicago, Chicago, IL
(1943.95)*

Grey Cross with Blue

1929, oil on canvas, 36 × 24 in.

*1983 and 1985 General Obligation Bonds,
Frederick R. Weisman Foundation, Overwest Corporation,
and the Albuquerque Museum Foundation
Purchase, The Albuquerque Museum, Albuquerque, NM
(85.50.1)*

Cebolla Church

1945, oil on canvas, 20 × 36⅛ in.

*Bequest of Robert F. Phifer in honor of Dr. Joseph C. Sloane,
North Carolina Museum of Art, Raleigh, NC*

Above:

Gate of Adobe Church

1929, oil on canvas, 20 1/16 × 16 in.

*Museum purchase: gift in memory of Elisabeth
Mellon Sellers from her friends,
The Carnegie Museum of Art, Pittsburgh, PA
(74.17)*

Top right:

In the Patio II

1948, oil on canvas, 18 × 30 in.

*Bequest of Helen Miller Jones, 1986,
Museum of Fine Arts, Museum of New Mexico,
Santa Fe, NM
(86.137.19)*

Bottom right:

In the Patio #1

1946, oil on paper, 30 × 24 in.

*Gift of Mr. and Mrs. Norton S. Walbridge,
San Diego Museum of Art, San Diego, CA
(1986:035)*

123

Above:

Wall with Green Door

1952, oil on canvas, 30 × 47⅞ in.

*Gift of the Woodward Foundation
In the Collection of The Corcoran Gallery of Art,
Washington, D.C.
(1977.8)*

Right:

Patio with Black Door

1955, oil on canvas, 40 × 30 in.

*Gift of the William H. Lane Foundation,
Courtesy of Museum of Fine Arts, Boston
(1990.433)*

Near Alcada, New Mexico
undated, oil on panel, 7 × 8¾ in.

Bequest of Doris M. Brixey,
Yale University Art Gallery, New Haven, CT
(1984.32.21)

Goat's Horn with Red

1945, pastel on paperboard, 27⅞ × 31¹¹⁄₁₆ in.

Gift of Joseph H. Hirshhorn, 1972,
Hirshhorn Museum and Sculpture Garden,
Smithsonian Institution, Washington, D.C.
(HMSG 72.217)

List of Color Plates

Artwork

PAGE 8 (TOP LEFT): **Portrait of Claudia**
1905, oil on canvas, 12×10 in.
Bequest of Claudia O'Keeffe, 1987,
Museum of Fine Arts, Museum of New
Mexico, Santa Fe, NM

PAGE 8 (TOP RIGHT): **My Auntie**
1905, ink on paper, 5½×5 in.
Bequest of Claudia O'Keeffe, 1987,
Museum of Fine Arts, Museum of New
Mexico, Santa Fe, NM

PAGE 10: **Seated Nude X**
1917, watercolor on paper, 11⅞×8⅞ in.
Van Day Truex Fund, 1981
The Metropolitan Museum of Art,
New York, NY

PAGE 13: **Red Barn, Lake George, New York**
1921, oil on canvas, 14×16¹⁄₁₆ in.
Eva Underhill Holbrook Memorial Collection of
American Art, Gift of Alfred H. Holbrook, The
University of Georgia, Georgia Museum of Art,
Athens, GA (GMOA 45.70)

PAGE 15: **New York, Night**
1928-29, oil on canvas, 40⅛×19⅛ in.
Thomas C. Woods Memorial Collection, 1958,
Sheldon Memorial Art Gallery, University of
Nebraska, Lincoln, NE

PAGE 17 (TOP): **Near Abiquiu, New Mexico**
1930, oil on canvas, 10×24⅛ in.
Alfred Stieglitz Collection, 1963,
The Metropolitan Museum of Art, New York,
NY (63.204)